PUFFIN BOOKS

Pillow Talk

Roger McGough was born in Liverpool and in the late sixties and
early seventies he was a member of the group The Scaffold.
Author of over thirty books for both children and adults, Roger
McGough has done much to popularize poetry. A frequent
broadcaster and an occasional playwright, he now lives in London.

'McGough manipulates, smoothes and bashes words into shapes
and notions that are guaranteed to thrill, delight, intrigue and
inform the soul' – *Books for Keeps*

PILLOW TALK
A BOOK OF POEMS

ROGER McGOUGH

ILLUSTRATIONS BY STEVEN GUARNACCIA

PUFFIN BOOKS

PUFFIN BOOKS

Published by the Penguin Group
Penguin Books Ltd, 27 Wrights Lane, London W8 5TZ
Penguin Books USA Inc., 375 Hudson Street, New York, New York 10014, USA
Penguin Books Australia Ltd, Ringwood, Victoria, Australia
Penguin Books Canada Ltd, 10 Alcorn Avenue, Toronto, Ontario, Canada M4V 3B2
Penguin Books (NZ) Ltd, 182–190 Wairau Road, Auckland 10, New Zealand

Penguin Books Ltd, Registered Offices: Harmondsworth, Middlesex, England

First published by Viking 1990
Published in Puffin Books 1992
9 10

Text copyright © Roger McGough, 1990
Illustrations copyright © Steven Guarnaccia, 1990
All rights reserved

The moral right of the author has been asserted

Filmset in Palatino

Printed in England by Clays Ltd, St Ives plc

This book I'd like to dedicate
To Philippa, Caroline and Kate.
Imran, Winston, Tom and Finn,
Ronnie, Susan, Björn and Lyn.

Liz, Markéta, Donna, Clare,
Running Deer and Jean-Pierre.
Hilary, Daisy, George and Paul,
Of course, to you most of all.

Vaclav, Spike, Satoshi, Scott,
(Whether they read the book or not).
Matti, Mark, Luke and John.
Get the picture? Everyone.

CONTENTS

PILLOW TALK

Last night I heard my pillow talk
What amazing things it said
About the fun that pillows have
Before it's time for bed

The bedroom is their playground
A magical place to be
(Not a room for peace and quiet
Like it is for you and me)

They divebomb off the wardrobe
Do backflips off the chair
Use the mattress as a trampoline
Turn somersaults in the air

It's Leapfrog then Pass the Slipper
Handstands and cartwheels all round
Wrestling and swinging on curtains
And all with hardly a sound

But by and by the feathers fly
And they get out of puff
So with scarves and ties they bind their eyes
For a game of Blind Man's Buff

They tiptoe out on the landing
Although it's a dangerous place
(If granny met one on the stairs
Imagine the look on her face!)

It's pillows who open cupboard drawers
To mess and rummage about
(And *you* end up by getting blamed
For something *they* left out)

I'd quite fancy being a pillow
Playing games and lying in bed
If I didn't have to spend each night
Under your big snoring head!

PILLOW FIGHT

As soon as my head
Hit the pillow
The pillow hit my head back

Hammering tongues
They were at it
Hammer and tongs

I sat up
And tried to separate them
But in vain

As soon as my head
Hit the pillow again
The pillow fought back

So I counted slowly
Up to ten
Then everything went black.

SICK BED

I rose from my sick bed
To write this verse
And sent for the doctor
When things got worse.

He took one look
Shook his head and said,
'No doubt about it
That's a very sick bed.

Give it a hot-water bottle
Three times a day
Keep it well wrapped up
Now I must be on my way.'

So I'm left here alone
With a sick bed to nurse
And nothing to do
But write a silly verse.

I'VE TAKEN TO MY BED

I've taken to my bed
(And my bed has taken to me)
We're getting married in the spring
How happy we shall be

We'll raise lots of little bunks
A sleeping-bag or two
Take my advice: find a bed that's nice
Lie down and say: 'I love you.'

YAWN

Never stifle a yawn
For doing what it's trained to do
One unsuspecting dawn
It might decide to stifle you.

LOVE STORY

One morning, a yawn
bored with the smug
dissatisfied face
that surrounded it

fled.

In Venice, crossing
the Bridge of Sighs
he met one, and
completely lost his

head.

A sigh for sore eyes
was she. So lovely
he popped the question.
No sooner said than

wed.

THE MIDNIGHT SKATERS

It is midnight in the ice-rink
    And all is cool and still.
Darkness seems to hold its breath
    Nothing moves, until

Out of the kitchen, one by one,
    The cutlery comes creeping,
Quiet as mice to the brink of the ice
    While all the world is sleeping.

Then suddenly, a serving-spoon
    Switches on the light,
And the silver swoops upon the ice
    Screaming with delight.

The knives are high-speed skaters
    Round and round they race,
Blades hissing, sissing,
    Whizzing at a dizzy pace.

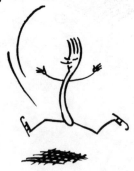

Forks twirl like dancers
   Pirouetting on the spot.
Teaspoons (who take no chances)
   Hold hands and giggle a lot.

All night long the fun goes on
   Until the sun, their friend,
Gives the warning signal
   That all good things must end.

So they slink back to the darkness
   Of the kitchen cutlery-drawer
And steel themselves to wait
   Until it's time to skate once more.

*

At eight the canteen ladies
   Breeze in as good as gold
To lay the tables and wonder
   Why the cutlery is so cold.

THE FIRST RUB OF DAWN

Glimpsed through the night
Is the glimmer of the day
Light is but darkness
Worn away.

SET IN ITS WAYS

If the sun didn't set
in the evening

But set
in the morning instead

We'd come home from school
after midnight

Have breakfast
then go straight to bed.

SNUGGGLES

Work done
for the day
the sun
switches on
the moon
pulls
the clouds
over its
head and
snugggles
right down
into the
cosy bottom
of the sky.

THE MISSING SOCK

I found my sock
beneath the bed.
'Where have you been
all week?' I said.

'Hiding away,'
the sock replied.
'Another day on your foot
and I would have died!'

TOP

Dad, risen and dizzy
from sleep, would say,
'I slept like a top.'

This puzzled me.
Top of what?
Top of the milk?
Top of the class?
Top of the wardrobe?
Top of the morning?

So I asked him.
'Spinning top,' he said.

Funny, I thought,
to spend all night
spinning round the bedroom.
No wonder he looked so tired every morning!

BOTTOM

Who'd be a bottom? Not me.

Always facing the wrong way.
To go for a walk
And not be able to see
Where you are going.

To be sat upon all day.
Smacked. Called rude names.
Whistled at. Laughed at.
The butt of a hundred jokes.

Faithful to the end.
An undercover agent
Working all hours
And getting no thanks for it.

Alas, poor bottom.

BUTTERING

When my little sister
wants something
she butters up my dad.

If she doesn't get it
she scrapes it all off
HARD!

ITCH

My sister had an itch
  I asked if it was catching.
'Catch,' she said, and threw it.
  Now I'm the one who's scratching.

WOULDN'T IT BE FUNNY IF YOU DIDN'T HAVE A NOSE?

You couldn't smell your dinner
If you didn't have a nose
You couldn't tell a dirty nappy
From a summer rose
You couldn't smell the ocean
Or the traffic, I suppose
Oh wouldn't it be funny
If you didn't have a nose?

You couldn't smell your mummy
If you didn't have a nose
You couldn't tell an orange
From a row of smelly toes
You couldn't smell the burning
(Think how quick a fire grows)
Wouldn't it be funny
If you didn't have a nose?

Where would we be without our hooters?
Nothing else would really suit us.
What would we sniff through?
How would we sneeze?
What would we wipe
Upon our sleeves?

You couldn't smell a rat
If you didn't have a nose
You couldn't tell a duchess
From a herd of buffaloes
And ... mmmm that Gorgonzola
As it starts to decompose
Oh wouldn't it be funny
If you didn't have a nose?

Where would we be without our hooters?
Nothing else would really suit us.
And think of those who
Rub their noses
Life would be tough for
Eskimoses.

You couldn't wear your glasses
If you didn't have a nose
And what would bullies aim for
When it came to blows?
Where would nostrils be without them?
When it's runny how it glows
Oh wouldn't it be funny
If you didn't have a ...
        have a ...
        have a ...
           a ...
           a ... choo!

SNEEZES

When I
sneeze

I don't go
'Achoo!'

Or
'Atishoo!'

I go
'Yar ... yar ... yar ... shar ... shar ... sh-sh-sh-ashkeroo!'

I don't think
my sneezes

ever learned
to spell.

I'VE GOT A COLD

I've got a cold
And it's not funny

My throat is numb
My nose is runny

My ears are burning
My fingers are itching

My teeth are wobbly
My eyebrows are twitching

My kneecaps have slipped
My bottom's like jelly

The button's come off
My silly old belly

My chin has doubled
My toes are twisted

My ankles have swollen
My elbows are blistered

My back is all spotty
My hair's turning white

I sneeze through the day
And cough through the night

I've got a cold
And I'm going insane

(Apart from all that
I'm as right as rain).

MOANY MARGARET

Moany Margaret
Day and night
One's too dark
One's too bright

Moany Margaret
Bread and honey
One's too chewy
One's too runny

Moany Margaret
Cello and flute
One's too stringy
One's too cute

Moany Margaret
Sea and sand
One's too wet
One's too bland

Moany Margaret
Cat and pony
One's too furry
One's too bony

Moany Margaret
Nat and Matty
One's too fat
One's too chatty

Moany Margaret
Mum and dad
One is gone
One is sad

Moany Margaret
So they name her
Margaret moans
Who can blame her?

TANTRUMS

When my sister starts to frown
I'm always on my guard

Yesterday she threw a tantrum
But it missed me by a yard.

SCOWLING

When I see you
scowling

I want to turn you
upside down

and see you
smile!

ANGELS ARE GOD'S MARINES

Angels are God's marines
A celestial SAS
Wherever there are ugly scenes
They go in and sort out the mess

Whenever there's a villain
And the war is going his way
(Like Hitler, for instance)
They're called in to save the day

From Waterloo to Wounded Knee
Orléans to Agincourt
They've changed the course of history
(That's what He trains them for)

Angels are God's marines
An elitist fighting force
You can volunteer to join them
(But you've got to be dead, of course).

INKLINGS

Summer
is just around the corner
they say.

Look
the inklings of a shadow.
Hooray!

THE SUN HAS GOT HIS HAT ON

The sun has got his hat on
Oh dear, oh dear, oh dear

It's a battered stetson
Which can only mean, I fear,

He wants to shoot it out
He's reaching for his gun

Counting slowly up to ten
And there's nowhere left to run.

PEELLY

Watch out for the sun
He's a strange one, really
Get too close
And he'll make you peelly.

WHEN TO CUT YOUR FINGERNAILS

Cut them on Monday
There's a good week ahead

Cut them on Tuesday
Better go straight to bed

Cut them on Wednesday
You're going to be rich

Cut them on Thursday
You might meet a witch

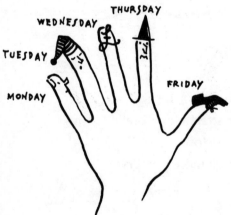

Cut them on Friday
You'll be walked off your feet

Cut them on Saturday
You're in for a treat

But cut them on Sunday
Without saying a prayer
And your nails will grow
As long as your hair!

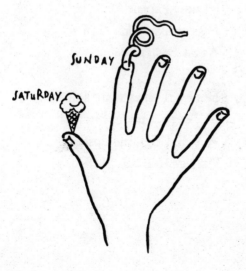

SID

How did you know
My name was Sid?
That's a fact
I've always hid.

When asked my name
I always say
'Tom' and look
The other way.

For reasons that
I'll now explain
I never liked Sid
As a Christian name.

Sidney rhymes with 'kidney'
So I keep it under my hat
And 'Sid, Sid, the dustbin lid'
I'm sick to death of that.

So how did you know
My name was Sid
Something
That I've always hid?

'Because it's tattooed on your forehead.'

THINKS SHE'S IT

Thinks she's it
    But she's not

Thinks she's good-looking
    But she isn't

Thinks she's got brains
    But she hasn't

Thinks I'll be her mate
    But I won't

Thinks I write poems about her
    But I don't.

INTRUDERS

What's nice is
when I'm left
to my own devices.

Getting on with things
in my own quiet way
or doing simply nothing,
not a thing all day.

But people have to interfere:
'Stop that! Do this!
No, not in here!' And all
for the sake of something to say.

Grown-up intruders.
When I grow up I hope
I'm not as rude as they.

THE SOUND COLLECTOR

A stranger called this morning
Dressed all in black and grey
Put every sound into a bag

And carried them away

The whistling of the kettle
The turning of the lock
The purring of the kitten
The ticking of the clock

The popping of the toaster
The crunching of the flakes
When you spread the marmalade
The scraping noise it makes

The hissing of the frying-pan
The ticking of the grill
The bubbling of the bathtub
As it starts to fill

The drumming of the raindrops
On the window-pane
When you do the washing-up
The gurgle of the drain

The crying of the baby
The squeaking of the chair
The swishing of the curtain
The creaking of the stair

A stranger called this morning
He didn't leave his name
Left us only silence
Life will never be the same.

CLING-FILM

I'm clingy
I cling
to any old thing
a sandwich, a shoe, whatever you bring

I'm clingy
I cling
you can see right through
and when I cling, I cling like glue

I'm clingy
I cling
and I'm coming for you
cling cling cling

Gotcha!

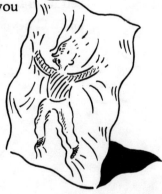

TUNA SANDWICHES

I want you
I want you
I want you
na sandwiches

I want you
I want you
I want you
na sandwiches

chew chew chew
na sandwiches

chew chew chew
na sandwiches.

PULL THE OTHER ONE

A crab, I am told,
　　will not bite
or poison you
　　just for spite.

Won't lie in wait
　　beneath a stone
until one morning,
　　out alone

You poke a finger
　　like a fool
into an innocent-
　　looking pool.

Won't leap out
   and grab your hand
drag you sideways
   o'er the sand

To the bottom
   of the sea
And eat you, dressed,
   for Sunday tea.

A crab, I am told,
   is a bundle of fun
(With claws like that
   Pull the other one.)

Ouch!

CROSS PORPOISES

The porpoises
were looking really cross
so I went over
and talked at them

Soon they cheered up
and swam away
leaving laughter-bubbles
in their wake

It never fails,
talking at cross porpoises.

GRUPER SOUP

Gruper soup
Gruper soup
I'm in a grupersoup

> I sing and swim
>   and play guitar
> I'm a gruper
>   superstar

Gruper soup
Gruper soup
I'm in a grupersoup

> All the fishes
>   in the band
> are the richest
>   in the land

Gruper soup
Gruper soup
I'm in a grupersoup

From Aberdeen
　　to Zanzibar
we're the grooviest
　　by far

Gruper soup
Gruper soup
I'm in a grupersoup

I'm delicious
　　I'm a treat
pick up a spoon
　　and drum out the beat

Gruper soup
Gruper soup
I'm in a gruper soup

GROUTS, GRUDS AND GRUMPLINGS

Keep your parsnips
Keep your sprouts
Give me heaps
Of buttered grouts

Grouts, grouts, grouts
    Are what vegies ought to be
Grouts, grouts, grouts
    They're the greens for me

Steam your cabbage
Boil your spuds
Give me plates
Of salty gruds

Grouts, grouts, gruds
    Are what vegies ought to be
Grouts, grouts, gruds
    They're the greens for me

Stuff your olives
Dump your dumplings
Give me loads
Of good old grumplings

Grouts, gruds and grumplings
　　Are what vegies ought to be
Grouts, gruds and grumplings
　　They're the greens for me.

LETTUCE LEAVES

When
lettuce leaves are old
lettuce leaves me cold

WHAT THE EARTH MUMBLED

'Mumble, mumble, mumble
I want my apple crumble.
If some crumble doesn't come
I'll grumble, grumble, grumble.'

WHAT THE MOON MUTTERED

'Mutter, mutter, mutter
I want my bread and butter
If some doesn't come real soon
I'll tut tut tut tut tutter.'

WHAT THE PLANETS SCOOBY DOOD

'Scooby dooby dooby do
We all want some Irish stew
Piping hot and thick as glue
Or we'll boo hoo, hoo hoo, hoo.'

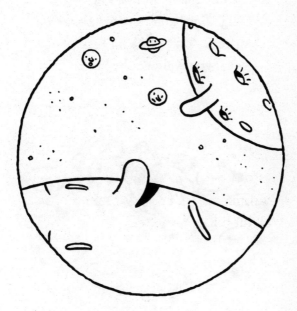

BUN FIGHT

The buns are having a fight
There are currants on the floor
The custards egg them on
'More,' they cry, 'more.'

The doughnuts form a ring
'Ding, ding!' and the seconds are out
An eccles cake is taking bets
As to who will win the bout.

The referee is a muffin
The time-keeper is a scone
There are five rounds still to go
And the custards egg them on.

The chelsea bun is tiring
And hoping for a draw
When the bath bun throws an uppercut
That brings him to the floor.

The muffin slowly counts him out
And the bath bun's arm is raised
While through the window, passers-by
Look into the cake-shop, amazed.

LOLLIDOLLOPS

I like a nice
dollop of ice-cream
on my porridge

I like a nice
dollop of ice-cream
in my tea

But the dollop
I like the most
is the one
I have on toast

With my eggs, bacon,
mushrooms, beans, sausages,
spaghetti, black puddings, spam fritters,
apple pie, mushy peas, tomatoes, kidneys and custard.

SWEETS FOR MY SWEET

Not only is she toffee-nosed
But she is ... bubblegum-mouthed
       candyfloss-haired
       polomint-eared
       chocolate-button-bellied
       smartie-pantsed
       and liquorice allsorts of things

In fact, she is very, very sweet.

SLOPPY TICKS

Why are kisses crosses
When you put them on a letter?
Big, juicy, sloppy ticks
Would be so much better.

THE BURP

One evening at supper
A little girl burped.
'Tut, tut,' said mother.
'What do you say?' said father.

Her brother giggled.
'It's not funny,' said father.
'Pardon,' said the little girl.
'That's better,' said mother.

And all was quickly forgotten.
Except, that is, by the burp.
It had only just been born
And already everybody was apologizing.

What sort of person gives birth
And then says 'pardon'?
What sort of relative giggles
Then looks away, embarrassed?

Hurt, the baby burp hovered near the ceiling
Looked down at the one who had brought it up
Then escaped through an open window,
Never to return.

GOING DOWN LIKE NINEPINS

... when suddenly, down the middle
of the crowded High Street
... thundered a Giant Wooden Ball!

Black and highly polished
it bounced off the buildings,
smashing windows and crushing cars.

People were going down like ninepins ...

ABC

Cars are really useful
for getting from A to B.
But I don't drive
and much prefer
to walk beside the C.

TREES ARE GREAT

Trees are great, they just stand and wait
They don't cry when they're teased
They don't eat much and they seldom shout
Trees are easily pleased

Trees are great, they like to congregate
For meetings in the park
They dance and sway, they stay all day
And talk till well after dark

Trees are great, they accept their fate
When it's pouring down with rain
They don't wear macs, it runs off their backs
But you never hear them complain

So answer me, please, if there weren't any trees
Where would naughty boys climb?
Where would lovers carve their names?
Where would little birds nest?
Where would we hang the leaves?

A-HUNTING WE WILL GO

A-hunting we will go
A-hunting we will go
In coats so gay and red

(On second thoughts
We hate blood sports
Let's go to the pictures instead).

THE HIPPOPOSTHUMOUS

The Hippoposthumous
is dead and gone

Pity the ground
he lays upon.

EARWIGS I

Earwigs wear earrings
When going to the ball

Roaches wear broaches
Or nothing at all.

EARWIGS II

Fancy having wigs for ears
That's the craziest invention for years!

What next? A hairpiece for a nose?
Or toupees for toes, I suppose?

THE KLEPTOMANIAC

Beware the Kleptomaniac
Who knows not wrong from right
He'll wait until you turn your back
Then steal everything in sight:

The nose from a snowman
(Be it carrot or coal)

The stick from a blindman
From the beggar his bowl

The smoke from a chimney
The leaves from a tree

A kitten's miaow
(Pretty mean you'll agree)

He'll pinch a used teabag
From out of the pot

A field of potatoes
And scoff the whole lot

(Is baby still there,
Asleep in its cot?)

He'll rob the baton
From a conductor on stage

All the books from the library
Page by page

He'll snaffle your shadow
As you bask in the sun

Pilfer the currants
From out of your bun

He'll lift the wind
Right out of your sails

Hold your hand
And make off with your nails

When he's around
Things just disappear

F nnily eno gh I th nk
Th re's one ar und h re!

HOBGOBLIN I

There is a hobgoblin
At the end of the street
Who wears hobnailed boots
On his hobnailed feet

On his hobnailed teeth
A hobnailed brace
A hobnailed mask
On his hobnailed face

A hobnailed glove
On his hobnailed fist
If he asks you out
Resist. Resist.

HOBGOBLIN II

I'm a hobgoblin
I hobble alone

Keep out of trouble
Do nobody harm

Children won't let me
Into their games

Point poisoned fingers
Call cruel names

I'm a hobgoblin
I hobble alone

On my wan and lonely
Woe begone own.

THE MAN WHO STEALS DREAMS

Santa Claus has a brother
A fact few people know
He does not have a friendly face
Or a beard as white as snow

He does not climb down chimneys
Or ride in an open sleigh
He is not kind and giving
But cruelly takes away

He is not fond of children
Or grown-ups who are kind
And emptiness the only gift
That he will leave behind

He is wraith, he is silent
He is greyness of steam
And if you're sleeping well tonight
Then hang on to your dream

He is sour, he is stooping
His cynic's cloak is black
And if he takes your dream away
You never get it back

Dreams with happy endings
With ambition and joy
Are the ones that he seeks
To capture and destroy

So, if you don't believe in Santa
Or in anything at all
The chances are his brother
Has already paid a call

THE ALL-PURPOSE CHILDREN'S POEM

The first verse contains a princess
    Two witches (one evil, one good)
There is a castle in it somewhere
    And a dark and tangled wood.

The second has ghosts and vampires
    Monsters with foul-smelling breath
It sends shivers down the book spine
    And scares everybody to death.

The third is one of my favourites
    With rabbits in skirts and trousers
Who talk to each other like we do
    And live in neat little houses.

The fourth verse is bang up to date
     And in it anything goes.
Set in the city, it doesn't rhyme
     (Although, in a way it does).

The fifth is set in the future
(And as you can see, it's the last)
When the Word was made Computer
And books are a thing of the past.

INDEX OF FIRST LINES